Countries Around the World
Chile

Marion Morrison

LIBRARY

Chicago, Illinois

©2012 Heinemann Library
an imprint of Capstone Global Library, LLC
Chicago, Illinois

Edited by Louise Galpine and Megan Cotugno
Designed by Ryan Frieson
Original illustrations © Capstone Global Library, Ltd., 2012
Illustrated by Oxford Designers & Illustrators
Picture research by Tracy Cummins
Originated by Capstone Global Library, Ltd.
Printed in China by China Translation and Printing Services

15 14 13 12 11
10 9 8 7 6 5 4 3 2 1

Library of Congress Cataloging-in-Publication Data
Morrison, Marion.

Chile / Marion Morrison.

p. cm.—(Countries around the world)

Includes bibliographical references and index.

ISBN 978-1-4329-5197-9 (hc)—ISBN 978-1-4329-5222-8 (pb)
1. Chile—Juvenile literature. I. Title.

F3058.5.M67 2012

983—dc22   2010043171

Acknowledgments

The author and publishers are grateful to the following for permission to reproduce copyright material: © AP Photo: p. 14 (Government of Chile, Hugo Infante); © Getty Images pp. 8 (CLAUDIO SANTANA/AFP), 9 (MARTIN BERNETTI/AFP), 13 (MARTIN BERNETTI/AFP), 19 (Tui De Roy), 28 (MARTIN BERNETTI/AFP), 29 (Travel Ink), 33 (Robert Francis); © istockphoto: p. 24 (© roccomontoya); © Photolibrary: p. 27 (Heiner Heine); © Shutterstock: pp. 5 (© Patrick Poendl), 11 (© Yoann Combronde), 12 (© N. Frey Photography), 16 (© Fotocrisis), 17 (© MARCELODLT), 38 (© Jansen.ATF), 46 (© granata1111); © South American Pictures: pp. 7, 18 (© Peter Francis), 23 (© Chris Sharp), 30 (© Tony Morrison), 34 (© Sue Mann); © Superstock: p. 15 (© Robert Harding Picture Library).

Cover photograph reproduced with permission of Corbis (© Momatiuk - Eastcott).

We would like to thank Richard Abisla for his invaluable help in the preparation of this book.

Contents

Some words in the book are in bold, **like this**. You can find out what they mean by looking in the glossary.

Introducing Chile

Chile is a long, narrow strip of land along the southwest coast of South America. It is tucked away in the shadow of the Andes mountains. In the north, it has one of the world's driest deserts, the Atacama. In the south, there are towering snow-capped mountains.

Ancient tribes

Monteverde, in southern Chile, is one of the oldest sites of human settlement in the world. There is evidence of 20 to 30 people living there possibly over 12,500 years ago. The early peoples were **nomadic**, hunting animals and fishing. Later, tribes like the Atacameños settled in the area. They grew crops, such as maize and beans, and kept animals, such as llamas and alpacas. Other peoples, such as the Mapuche, continued to hunt and fish in the southern forests and also farmed. In the far south, tribes such as the Chono people lived on the windswept, freezing plains. From their canoes, they used arrows to hunt seals, otters, and birds. They wore animal skins to protect themselves against the cold.

Easter Island

Chile owns Easter Island in the Pacific Ocean, one of the world's most remote islands. It is famous for huge stone statues that are hundreds of years old. They were carved by Polynesian people who came and settled from islands in the west Pacific, but no one knows why.

CHINCHORRO MUMMIES

In 1983 workmen discovered several **mummies** in the Atacama desert. They belonged to the Chinchorro people. The Chinchorro had a special way of preserving the bodies of their dead. These mummies, over 5,000 years old, are the oldest mummies in the world.

These three peaks in the Torres del Paine National Park in Patagonia are known as the Towers of Paine.

History:
From Colony to Country

In the 1400s, the Incas, rulers of a vast empire north of Chile, conquered most Chilean tribes. In 1520 Portuguese explorer Ferdinand Magellan sailed around southern Chile through the passage now called the Strait of Magellan. Early in the 1530s, Spanish soldiers destroyed much of the Inca Empire. They invaded Chile first in 1536, and then again in 1540. In 1541 the Spanish general, Pedro de Valdivia, founded Santiago, Chile's capital city. Like the Incas, the Spaniards were also unable to conquer the Mapuche tribe in the south. The Spanish settled in the north where they began to farm, and their **colony** lasted almost 300 years.

Independence

By the early 1800s, many colonists wanted **independence** from Spain. One of their leaders was Bernardo O'Higgins. In 1817 he became the Supreme Director of Chile, like a president. In 1818, after several battles, Spanish forces were defeated at the Battle of Maipú. Chile became an independent country.

In the 1800s, Chile prospered when deposits of guano—bird droppings—and nitrate salts in the Atacama were sold overseas as **fertilizers**. A disagreement over control of the nitrate deposits led to the War of the Pacific (1879–1883) when Chile defeated neighboring Peru and Bolivia. In the 1880s, government troops overcame the Mapuche and controlled the whole country for the first time.

BERNARDO O'HIGGINS (1778–1842)

Bernardo O'Higgins was the son of an Irish father and Spanish mother. As Supreme Director (1817—1823) he founded colleges and libraries, the navy, and improved the army. His enemies forced him from office in 1823, and he died in Peru.

Bernardo O'Higgins served as the first president of Chile from 1817 to 1823.

The 1900s

For years Chileans demanded better working and living conditions. But it was only in the 1960s that President Eduardo Frei set about resolving these problems. Salvador Allende succeeded him in 1970. His government took over many industries and broke up large farms to give land to the poor. This left the country with huge debts.

President Allende was **deposed** by the army chief, General Augusto Pinochet. He was a **dictator** who held power from 1973 to 1989. Thousands of people who opposed his military **regime** were killed or tortured. His government did, however, improve the economy. Mass protests led to new presidential elections in 1989, won by Patricio Aylwin. In 2006 Michelle Bachelet became the first female president. Sebastián Piñera won the 2010 elections.

Chileans

Most Chileans are descendants of both **immigrants** and native peoples. The first immigrants were Spanish and more came from the **Basque** country in the 1700s. Other Europeans and people from the Middle East followed. From the 1850s, large numbers of Germans settled in the south. More recently immigrants have arrived from other South American countries.

Chilean teenagers hang out outside of a nightclub in Santiago.

Ethnic Groups of Chile

White and white-Native American	Mapuche	Other indigenous groups
95.4%	4%	0.6%

CIA: 2002 census

Native peoples

The Mapuche are the largest native group. Most make a poor living selling handicrafts or finding temporary work on farms or in towns. The Aymara are a much smaller group and also very poor. They live in the mountains, growing a few crops for local markets. The tribes of the far south died out when settlers and sheep farmers arrived.

A Mapuche father with his son.

Regions and Resources: Country of Contrasts

Chile is about 4,300 kilometers (2,700 miles) long. The **Tropic of Capricorn** crosses the north while its southern tip is only 644 kilometers (400 miles) from the Antarctic. Its widest point is 349 kilometers (217 miles), and its narrowest about 16 kilometers (10 miles). Chile shares its northern border with Peru. The Andes Mountains run the length of Chile. They form the frontier with Bolivia in the northeast and Argentina in the east. They are part of a huge mountain chain that runs for 8,851 kilometers (5,500 miles) down the west of South America.

Chile has a long coastline facing the Pacific Ocean. Its islands include Chiloé, Juan Fernández, and Easter Island. It shares the island of Tierra del Fuego in the south with Argentina.

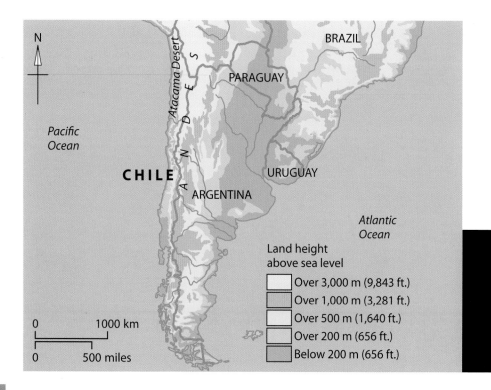

This map shows the different elevations of Chile.

The northern region

The Atacama Desert covers much of northern Chile, from sea level to the foothills of the Andes. Ojos del Salado, the world's highest active volcano at 6,887 meters (22,614 feet), is here. The Atacama, though very dry, is often very foggy. It seldom rains, and some places have never seen rain. The Loa is the only river that crosses the desert. It creates a fertile valley where people live and farm.

The central region

The central region extends south from the Atacama to near the Bío-Bío river. It has the richest farmland in the country. The climate is mild and free of frost. Much of the original forest has been replaced with vineyards and orchards. Santiago and many of Chile's largest cities are in this region.

Volcanoes overlook the *puna*, or high grasslands, of the Atacama Desert.

The south

Southern Chile is divided between the Lake District and Patagonia in the far south. The Lake District is a spectacular wonderland of forests, lakes, waterfalls, and volcanoes. Some volcanoes, such as the perfectly cone-shaped Osorno, are often covered in snow. Others are active with craters of red-hot lava. Green fields have replaced much of the original forest. Towns founded by **immigrants** have buildings that are very similar to those in parts of Germany.

Puntiagudo, or "sharp-pointed," volcano in Chile's Lake District.

Patagonia

Patagonia is the name of the southern region of Chile and Argentina. It is a land covered in ice, snow, and glaciers. Along the Chilean coast there are dozens of **fjords**, and small, uninhabited islands. At a high level, Patagonia is covered by so much ice that the far south is cut off from the rest of the country. Glaciers stream down into blue-green lakes. Experts are concerned that the glaciers are getting smaller as the Earth's temperature is warming.

Daily Life

An earthquake in February 2010 rocked Chile, with tremors felt in Argentina and Peru. Towns and villages along the coast were destroyed and the entire city of Concepción was moved 3 meters (10 feet) to the west. Most of Chile's buildings are designed to survive earthquakes. This saved the lives of many hundreds of people. Even so, 700 people died. In 1960, in Chile's biggest earthquake of the 20th century, nearly 2,000 people were killed.

Buildings in Concepción were destroyed in the earthquake of February 2010.

Mining

Chile's mineral resources include copper, gold, silver, iron, and semi-precious gems. Two of the world's largest copper mines, Chuquicamata and El Teniente, are in Chile. Copper provides about one-third of the government's **revenue**. Chile also has coal, oil, and gas reserves. It has more industries than most countries in South America. They produce textiles, cars, steel, cement, household goods, and food products.

Chilean miner rescue

On August 5, 2010, an accident left thirty-three Chilean miners trapped over a half-mile underground. They survived in the underground mine for over two months, before a dramatic rescue that was watched around the world on television.

Rescued miner Richard Villaroel waves a Chilean flag after being rescued from the collapsed San Jose gold and copper mine near Copiapo, Chile, October 13, 2010.

Castro is the capital of Chiloé. The church of San Francisco is on the top of the hill.

Adventurous landscapes and islands

Chile has many spectacular landscapes to attract tourists, but young tourists especially enjoy the adventure-packed vacations. Chile offers skiing, hiking, and white-water rafting.

Many tourists visit the Chiloé islands, famous for the 150 wooden churches dating from the 1700s to the 1800s. Largely ignored by people on the mainland during colonial times, the Chiloé settlers, **missionaries**, and islanders developed their own culture. They even have their own form of Spanish. The culture involves many **superstitions** and a belief in witchcraft ghost ships, and forest gnomes.

Daily Life

The currency used in Chile is the peso. There are coins of 5, 10, 50, 100, and 500 pesos and paper currency notes of 1,000, 2,000, 5,000, 10,000, and 20,000 pesos.

Producing food and wine

Vines were first brought to Chile in the 1500s. Today, Chile is one of the world's main **exporters** of wine. Chile also **exports** many different fruits and vegetables. Beef and dairy cattle are bred in the central valley while much of the sheep rearing takes place on huge farms in Patagonia and Tierra del Fuego.

Fishing and forestry

Chile has a large fishing industry, catching all kinds of fish and shellfish, including mackerel, anchovy, and eels. Some scientists worry that the fishing fleets may be catching too much and that some **species** may be endangered. Because of this, the government has imposed controls to protect the fish stocks.

Vineyards can be seen on hilly slopes in the central valley.

The fishing industry is important to Chile.

"ROBINSON CRUSOE"

Isla Robinson Crusoe and Isla Alexander Selkirk are the two main Juan Fernández islands. They are named after a Scottish sailor, Alexander Selkirk, who was stranded there for four years and four months in 1704, with only his Bible and wild goats for company. His story inspired Daniel Defoe to write the book *Robinson Crusoe*. Today, about 600 people live on Robinson Crusoe. Lobster fishing is the island's main industry.

Wildlife:
A Land of Many Habitats

The desert, mountains, forests, coast, and icy regions of Chile offer a great variety of habitat, but there is not a wide range of wildlife. The Andes are a natural barrier to animals migrating (moving) from other parts of South America. The Atacama is mostly dry, but occasionally it rains, and then the desert bursts into a mass of pink flowers. In higher parts, flamingos, and other waterbirds live on salt lakes. A bird called the rhea, which is similar to an ostrich, survives on the *puna*, or high grasslands, where tough plants have adapted to the higher altitude.

The Atacama Desert is at an altitude of about 2,500 meters (over 8,000 feet). Rain occasionally causes beautiful flowers to grow.

Daily Life

High in the Andes, boys and girls herd llamas and alpacas, animals which provide them with wool and meat. They are related to the wild *vicuña* and *guanaco*. The *vicuña* were almost hunted to extinction for their wool and meat. They are now protected. *Guanaco* are common in Patagonia.

Winter in the Malacahuello National Reserve sees the monkey puzzle trees covered in snow.

Forests

Forests, natural and planted, cover about 20 percent of the country. Most of the **plantations** are pine and eucalyptus. The wood is used for exports, such as woodchips, pulp, paper, and furniture.

Chile's southern rain forest is **temperate** or cool, not **tropical**. There are only four other similar forests left in the world. One of the **species** of trees native to Chile is the monkey puzzle pine. The story is that an Englishman in the 1800s said that the tree would be "a puzzle for a monkey to climb."

Forest animals include pumas and the pudu, the world's smallest deer. In Tierra del Fuego, the forests are home to the native Fuegian fox. The island also has many species of bird, including albatrosses, penguins, and geese. Along the coast, the most common sea mammals are sea lions, dolphins, and different species of whales.

A polluted capital

Santiago is one of the world's most **polluted** cities. Factories, industries, and hundreds of thousands of cars emit gases, smoke, and particles into the air. The city is in a valley, surrounded by mountain ranges. Its location, together with some unique weather patterns, keeps the **pollution** from escaping. The city is often covered in gray **smog**. Its people suffer from breathing difficulties. The government has tried to reduce the number of vehicles and temporarily close industries, but smog is still a major problem.

In the Atacama Desert, emissions from mines contribute to air pollution. Mining has also damaged the water supply and some local people have experienced pains and skin problems.

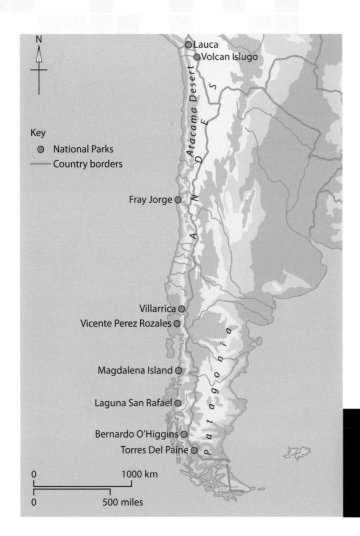

This map shows the location of Chile's national parks.

National parks

Chile's national parks provide places where **eco-tourists** can see and learn about wildlife, without harming the environment. The temperate forest, the *alerce*, is now protected by law. Some of the alerce are about 4,000 years old and are among the oldest trees in the world. The wood is of great value and so much has been cut down that few trees have survived. In Patagonia the Laguna San Rafael National Park contains the impressive San Rafael Glacier, 70 meters (300 feet) high, where it enters the San Rafael lake.

Infrastructure: Living and Learning

Chile is a **democracy** governed by a president, a congress which makes the laws, and courts which enforce the laws. The president is elected for four years, but cannot immediately run again for a second term. The Congress is made up of a Senate with 38 senators elected for 8 years, and a House of Deputies with 120 members who serve for 4 years. Everyone over the age of 18 must vote.

The country is divided into 14 regions and the Santiago Metropolitan Region. The regions are divided into provinces and the provinces into smaller districts, known as communes. The regions are governed by an official called an *intendant*, the provinces by a governor, and the communes by a mayor and a group of councilors elected for four years. Chile is a member of many international organizations, including the **United Nations**.

This map shows the 14 regions of Chile.

Congress moved to the Congress Building in Valparaiso from Santiago in 1990.

The Chilean National Anthem

The national anthem of Chile is known as the "Himno Nacional."

Pure, Chile, is your blue sky;
Pure breezes cross you as well.
And your flower-embroidered field
Is the happy copy of Eden.
Majestic is the white mountain
That was given to you as a bastion by the Lord
That was given to you as a bastion by the Lord
And that sea that calmly washes your shores
Promises you a future splendor
And that sea that calmly washes your shores
Promises you a splendid future.

Sweet fatherland, accept the vows
With which Chile swore at your altars:
Either the tomb of the free will you be
Or the refuge against oppression.

Daily Life

Around 5.4 million people live in Santiago. It is one of Latin America's most modern cities with dozens of elegant shopping malls, theaters, outdoor cafes, museums, and art galleries. There are skyscrapers, a subway system, and bicycle trails.

Living in Chile

About 90 percent of Chile's population lives in the central valley, and almost 90 percent of these live in cities and towns. Many families have moved from rural areas in search of work, better medical care, and schooling.

Housing and health

Some of Chile's most unusual houses are the rows of colorful wooden-stilted *palafitos* in Chiloé. But most people live in brick-built houses or high-rise apartment blocks, and the government has built small units of public housing for working people. **Shantytowns**, or slums, have grown up around many cities. The conditions are very basic with limited clean water and **sanitation**. This can lead to health problems, although Chilean children are vaccinated against the most common diseases like measles or mumps. Chile is number 32 on the **World Health Organization's** list of best health systems.

These *palafitos*, or stilted houses, are built above water level in Castro, Chiloé.

A woman's role

Until 1949 Chilean women were not allowed to vote, but in 2006, Michelle Bachelet became president of Chile. Education has made a great difference to the lives of women. Today, women do every kind of work from politics to apple-picking. Women are able to work because relatives help look after the children. In wealthier households, poorer people are paid to work as domestic servants.

YOUNG PEOPLE

"A Roof for Chile" is a program in which about 15,000 student volunteers spend their vacations building emergency housing—wooden shacks— for slum dwellers. It has been a great success. The number of families living in slums has dropped from 106,000 in 1996 to 20,000 families in 2009.

This map shows the population density of Chile.

People per square kilometer
- 10–100
- 1–10
- Under 1

Going to school

Chilean children aged six to fourteen must attend elementary school, and then secondary school until they are eighteen. Everyone has to wear a school uniform. The style of skirts, blouses, sweaters, pants, and shirts is similar, but each school can choose its own colors. Children greet their school friends with a hug or cheek kiss. The classes include geography, science, art, and languages. An "English Opens Doors" program encourages students of all ages to learn English. Sports are generally an after-school activity. Over 95 percent of Chileans over age 15 can read and write.

Staying in touch

About half the population have computers or use **cybercafés**. These are particularly popular with students for games and social networking. Most schools now have Internet access, but not all teachers know how to use computers. During the 2010 earthquake, cell phones were often the only means of communication for people trapped in the dark with no fixed phone, Internet, or television connection. Sometimes there were problems with the cellphone service, too.

How to say...

Most Chileans speak Spanish, though there are also native languages. The Mapuche language is *Mapudungun*, the Aymara language is called *Aymara*, and the Polynesians of Easter Island speak *Rapa Nui*. Native languages are slowly changing as more children learn Spanish as a first language and then mix the two. English and German are also spoken. Here are the numbers one to five in Spanish and two other Chilean languages:

Spanish	Rapa Nui	Mapudungun
Uno	*(ka) tahi*	*kiñe*
Dos	*(ka) rua*	*epu*
Tres	*(ka) toru*	*küla*
Cuatro	*(ka) ha*	*meli*
Cinco	*(ka) rima*	*kechu*

Young boys and girls are at
school in Santiago.

Culture:
Leisure Time and the Arts

You can reach the coast or the mountains within a few hours from anywhere in Chile. Viña del Mar is the main coastal resort near Santiago. While children can sail and surf, the water is too cold for swimming. Chile's main ski resort, Portillo, is close to Santiago. Families also spend days in the mountains walking and climbing.

Young people can get involved in many sports in Chile, but soccer is the most popular. Two of the best-known players are Marcelo Salas, who is the leading goal scorer for the national team, and Iván Zamorano.

Boys start learning to surf at a very young age.

YOUNG PEOPLE

In Chile young people and their parents enjoy kite flying. They buy kites or make their own from balsa wood and tissue paper. The aim is to see who can fly their kite longest and highest. They also have competitions where kites "fight" each other in flight. Some even coat their strings in glass to make it easier to cut the strings on other kites.

Rodeos

Rodeos originated from the time when Chilean cowboys, *huasos*, rounded up cattle. They traditionally dress in large-brimmed hats, colorful striped **ponchos**, and high-heeled leather boots with large silver **spurs**. Today's rodeos draw crowds of spectators. They are a chance for *huasos* to show off their skills, riding magnificent horses and controlling cattle. There are local rodeos and national championships.

Horsemen catch cattle at a rodeo in the south of the country.

Food and markets

Chileans buy much of their food in supermarkets. For many Chileans, lunchtime is when they eat their main meal of the day. Soups and stews based on fish are popular, particularly *caldillo de congrio*—eel soup with potatoes and onions. Potatoes and corn are the basic foods in many households. *Humitas*, mashed corn wrapped in corn husks and then steamed, are a family favorite. One of the most unusual dishes, *curanto*, comes from Chiloé. This mix of meat, shellfish, and vegetables is cooked in large leaves on hot coals in a hole in the ground.

Daily Life

In the summer, families and friends love to have a kind of barbecue called an *asado* with sausages, ribs, steak, or other meats cooked on a grill. Another traditional form of barbecue is the *asado al palo* when whole animals are spread over wooden sticks nailed into the ground facing a fire of burning coals. *Asados* are eaten with salads, and a sauce of mashed garlic and hot peppers.

This dish is called Pastel de Choclo (Corn Pie). See the recipe on the next page for how to make it!

Pastel de Choclo (Corn Pie)

This recipe is enjoyed by many Chileans. Ask an adult to help you with chopping, cooking with hot oil, and taking the cooked dish out of the oven.

Ingredients:

- 2 medium onions, finely chopped
- 2 hard-boiled eggs, sliced
- 3 garlic cloves, pressed, peeled and thinly sliced
- 1 tablespoon sweet Hungarian paprika
- 8 to 10 pitted whole black olives
- 1 tablespoon ground cumin and ½ teaspoon dried oregano

- 2 tablespoons olive oil
- ½ cup black raisins
- 1 pound ground beef OR skinless, boneless chicken, chopped in small cubes
- 2 16-ounce cans of cut corn, drained
- 1 cup chopped tomatoes
- 2 eggs
- salt, pepper, basil

What to do:

1. Lightly fry the onions, garlic, paprika, and cumin in the olive oil in a medium frying pan.

2. After about 5 minutes, add the ground beef or chicken and sauté until cooked through.

3. Add the tomatoes and oregano. Cover and simmer for 15 to 20 minutes, stirring occasionally.

4. Spread the meat mixture evenly over bottom of an oven proof dish.

5. Spread the hard-boiled egg slices evenly over the meat mixture. Arrange the olives in rows, and press gently into the meat. Sprinkle with the raisins.

6. In a blender puree the corn with the raw eggs, basil, and salt. Spread evenly over the top of mixture.

7. Bake, uncovered, at 350°F for 45 minutes or until lightly browned on top and firm, but moist.

Religion and festivals

Most Chileans are **Catholics**, the religion brought from Spain in the 1500s by **missionaries**. Public holidays are mostly Catholic celebrations, but a new holiday, Reformation Day, was introduced in 2008 for non-Catholic Christians, such as **Protestants** and **Evangelicals**. Other Chileans follow **Judaism** and **Islam**.

Percentage of followers of different religions in Chile

Roman Catholic	Evangelical	Jehovah's Witness	Other Christian	Other	None
70%	15%	1%	1%	4.6%	8.3%

CIA: 2002 census

Daily Life

The Mapuche, Aymara, and the people of Chiloé have their own spiritual beliefs, which they sometimes mix with the Catholic religion. They believe their gods live in the natural world around them. Spiritual healers perform ceremonies for curing diseases and warding off evil. The Mapuche spiritual healer is known as a *Machi* and is usually a woman.

Other celebrations

Chileans celebrate Independence Day on September 18 with street parties, music, and dancing. The largest religious festival is in La Tirana in the far north. Thousands of **pilgrims** and hundreds of costumed masked dancers take part. The festival celebrates an Inca princess who fell in love with a Spanish soldier and became a Christian so she could marry him. But this angered her people who killed her and her lover.

The *Domingo de Cuasimodo* festival on the first Sunday after Easter dates back to a time when *huasos* rode with priests to save them from being robbed by bandits. In the festival, *huasos*, including children, dress in traditional costume and parade through the streets on horseback, alongside a priest sitting on a float covered in white lilies.

Riders of all ages take part in the Festival of Cuasimodo.

Chile Today

Throughout its history and continuing today, the people of Chile have celebrated their culture and ancient traditions.

Here, a *huaso* in traditional dress dances the *cueca* with his partner.

Music

The music of Chile has Spanish, Andean, and native roots, with instruments such as the guitar, panpipes, and flutes. Mapuche instruments include a long horn made of bamboo and a cow's horn, and a small bowl-shaped drum made of leather. The *cueca* is the national dance. The steps represent the courtship of a man and woman, who dance twirling kerchiefs in the air.

Literature

Chileans have also fought for progress in their country through music and literature. In 1945 the Chilean poet Gabriela Mistral was the first **Latin American** to win the **Nobel Prize for Literature**. Her poems were about everyday life, love, and sorrow. Pablo Neruda won his Nobel Prize in 1971. Much of his poetry had political themes. Isabel Allende, a relative of the former president Salvador Allende, is perhaps Chile's best-known writer.

VICTOR JARA (1932–1973)

Singer-songwriter Victor Jara was brought up in a Santiago slum. In the 1960s, he joined other musicians in the New Song Movement. Their songs about poverty, **human rights**, and injustice brought the singers into conflict with the military government. General Pinochet banned their music. Some of the musicians were **exiled**, and Victor Jara was arrested, tortured, and shot.

Looking to the future

The military dictatorship of the 1970s and 1980s and its harsh measures shocked the people of Chile who previously had known only peaceful, democratically elected governments. But when **democracy** returned in 1989 the **economy** was strong, based on the natural resources that are the key to Chile's survival. Chile entered the 21st century as one of South America's richest and most stable nations.

Fact File

Country Name: Republic of Chile

Capital: Santiago

Languages: Spanish, Mapudungun, German, English, Rapa Nui

Population: 16,601,707

Life Expectancy: average 77.34 years

Religion: Roman Catholic 70%, Evangelical 15.1%, Jehovah's Witness 1%, other Christian 1%, other 4.6%, none 8.3%

Type of Government: Republic

Independence Date: September 18, 1810

National Symbols: condor, huemal (deer), and copihue flower

National Anthem: "Himno Nacional de Chile"

Climate: temperate; desert in north; Mediterranean in central region; cool and damp in south

Total Area: 756,102 square kilometers (292,260 square miles)

Bordering Countries: Argentina, Bolivia, Peru

Coast: 6,435 kilometers (3,996 miles)

Major Landforms: low coastal mountains, fertile central valley, Andes in east

Major Rivers: Loa, Bío-Bío, Copiapo, Maipo

Highest Elevation: Nevado Ojos del Salado, 6,880 meters (22,573 feet)

Lowest Elevation: Pacific Ocean, 0 meters (sea level)

Currency: Chilean pesos

Resources: copper, timber, iron ore, nitrates, semi-precious gems

Imports: petroleum and petroleum products, chemicals, electrical and telecommunications equipment, industrial machinery, vehicles, natural gas

Exports: copper, fruit, fish products, paper and pulp, chemicals, wine

Major Industries: foodstuffs, fish, processing, iron and steel, wood, products, transport, equipment, cement, textiles

Agricultural Products: grapes, apples, pears, onions, wheat, corn, oats, peaches, garlic, asparagus, beans, beef, poultry, wool, fish, timber

Largest Cities: Santiago (population 5,428,590)
Valparaíso (population 803,683)
Concepción (population 666,381)

National Holidays:

January 1	New Years Day
March/April	Easter
May 1	Labor Day
May 21	Navy Day
July 16	Our Lady of Mount Carmel
August 15	Assumption of Mary
September 18	Independence Day
October 12	Columbus Day
October 31	Reformation Day
November 1	All Saints
December 8	Immaculate Conception
December 25	Christmas Day

Fish is sold at the market in Valdivia.

Famous Chileans:

Isabel Allende (b. 1942), novelist

Salvador Allende (1908–1973), president 1970–1973

Patricio Aylwin (b. 1918), president 1990–1994

Michelle Bachelet (b. 1951),
  first female President 2006–2010

Eduardo Frei (1911–1982), president 1964–1970

Victor Jara (1932–1973),
  theater director, singer, songwriter

Gabriela Mistral (1889–1957),
  poet and Nobel Prize winner

Pablo Neruda (1904–1973),
  poet and Nobel Prize winner

Bernardo O'Higgins (1778–1842),
  Supreme Director of Chile 1817–1823

Angel Parra (b. 1943), musician

Isabel Parra (b. 1939), musician

Augusto Pinochet (1915–2006),
  president and army commander 1973–1990

Marcelo Salas (b. 1974), soccer player

Iván Zamorano (b. 1967), soccer player

Timeline

BCE means "before the common era." When this appears after a date it, refers to the number of years before the Christian religion began. BCE dates are always counted backward.

CE means "common era." When this appears after a date, it refers to the time after the Christian religion began.

BCE

c. 12,500	Humans settle at Monteverde
c. 5000	Native peoples in area of Chile are settling into communities and growing crops

CE

late 1400s	Incas invade
c. 1520	Ferdinand Magellan discovers southern passage around South America
1536	Spanish soldier Diego de Almagro enters Chile
1541	Pedro de Valdivia conquers most of Chile and founds Santiago
1554	Mapuche defeat the Spanish, destroy their forts, and Pedro de Valdivia is killed
1700s	First Basque settle in Chile
1818	Battle of Maipú—royalist forces are defeated and Chile wins independence
1817–1823	Bernardo O'Higgins is Supreme Director of Chile
1840–1850s	Large numbers of European immigrants arrive
1879–1883	Chile defeats Bolivia and Peru in War of the Pacific
1880s	Government troops subdue Mapuche Indians
1883–1901	More European immigrants arrive

1960	World's most powerful recorded earthquake hits coast near Valdivia
1964–1970	President Eduardo Frei attempts social reform
1970	Salvador Allende is elected president
1973–1989	Military rule under General Augusto Pinochet
1989	In democratic elections Patricio Alywin is elected president
2006	First female president, Michelle Bachelet Jeria, elected
2010	Sebastián Piñera is elected president
2010	Earthquake kills about 700 people
2010	33 miners are trapped for over two months in the San Jose mine in Copiapo

Glossary

Basque European people whose homeland is in southern France and northern Spain. They have their own language and culture.

Catholic Christian who follows the Roman Catholic Church headed by the pope

colony territory that is governed by another country

cybercafé cafe whose customers sit at computer terminals and log on to the Internet

democracy form of government in which the power lies with the people

depose remove from political office, usually by force

descendant person from an ancestor

dictator ruler who assumes complete power

eco-tourism tourism that protects the environment, its animals, and plants

economy organizational structure of goods and services in a country

exiled removed by force from your country of origin

evangelical protestant churches who base their teaching on the gospel

export good or service sold by one country to other countries

fertilizer substance added to soil to help plants grow

fjord long, narrow inlet of the sea between steep slopes or cliffs

human rights basic rights many believe all people deserve

immigrant person who moves from one country to another to live there

import goods and services bought by one country from other countries

independence governing of a country by its own people

Islam religion that follows the teachings of Mohammed

Judaism Jewish religion

Latin America areas of North and South America where Spanish or Portuguese is spoken

missionary someone who works overseas for their religion

mummy dead body that has been preserved

Nobel Prize for Literature prize given annually by the Nobel Foundation for excellence and contribution to world literature

nomadic moving from place to place

pilgrim someone who travels to a particular place for religious reasons

plantation large areas of land where crops are grown

pollution human-made waste

poncho garment to cover the upper body, made from a square of material with a hole for the head

Protestant Christian religion that does not recognize the authority of the pope

regime another word for government

republic form of government with an elected leader

revenue money made through an activity

sanitation water and sewage system

shantytown slum settlement on the edge of a city

smog combination of the words "smoke" and "fog" to mean thick air pollution

species particular types of animals or plants

spur sharp metal piece attached to a horse rider's heel

superstition belief based on fear or ignorance

temperate having a mild temperature all year

tropical hot and humid

Tropic of Capricorn imaginary line circling Earth south of the Equator at latitude 23.27 degrees

United Nations international organization that promotes peace, security, and cooperation

World Health Organization agency body of the United Nations that works to improve and promote world health

Find Out More

Books

Burgan, Michael. *Chile. (Enchantment of the Wolrd.)* New York: Children's Press, 2010.

Dipiazza, Francesca Davis. *Chile in Pictures. (Visual Geograhy.)* Minneapolis: Twenty-First Century Books, 2007.

Morrison, Marion. *Countries of the World: Chile.* New York: Facts on File, 2005.

Ryan, Pam Munoz. *The Dreamer.* New York: Scholastic, 2010.

Shields, Charles J. *Chile. (South America Today.)* Philadelphia: Mason Crest Publishers, 2009.

Websites

www.travelforkids.com/Funtodo/Chile/chile.htm

This website lists books to read and places to visit in Chile.

www.bbc.co.uk/news/10119130

This web article describes a project, after the 2010 earthquake, set up to give students access to computers while traveling to school by bus.

www.mtu.edu/news/stories/2010/march/story23904.html

In these news stories children write about their experience of the 2010 earthquake.

www.bbc.co.uk/worldservice/news/2010/03/100303_robinson_crusoe_island_wt_sl.shtml

This website explains how a 12-year-old girl helped save many lives on the island of Robinson Crusoe.

Places to visit

Santiago: Take the ride by funicular to the top of Cerro San Cristobal and get a panoramic view of the city. Then make the return trip by cable car.

Torres del Paine: This is in a national park in the far south and is perhaps the most stunning landscape in Chile. You can go on short walks or long hikes and admire the amazing mountain scenery.

San Pedro de Atacama: This is a small town in the Atacama and the best place from which to explore higher parts of the desert. From San Pedro you can visit the huge salt lakes with rare flamingos, the Valley of the Moon with weird sand and rock formations, and the Tatio Geysers which send billowing clouds of steam high in the air.

Easter Island: This is a long way to go, about five hours by plane from Santiago, but worth it to see the giant statues, or moai, built hundreds of years ago and still mysterious.

Topic Tools

You can use these topic tools for your school projects. Trace the flag and map on to a sheet of paper, using the thick black outlines to guide you, then color in your pictures. Make sure you use the right colors for the flag!

The Chilean Flag is similar to the Texas State Flag: a lone star on a blue background, and red and white stripes. The blue is for the sky, white for the snow-capped Andes, and red for the blood of dead soldiers. The star represents progress and honor.

■ Santiago

Index

Titles in the series